To Maira,

Fierce Light

Poets Respond to the Centenary
of the Battle of the Somme

*Yrsa Daley-Ward, Jackie Kay,
Bill Manhire, Paul Muldoon &
Daljit Nagra*

Gatehouse Press

Published by
Gatehouse Press Limited
32 Grove Walk
Norwich NR1 2QG
www.gatehousepress.com

ISBN 978-0-9934748-2-8

About Gatehouse Press:

Gatehouse Press is an independent publisher based in Norwich, UK; our core mission
is to give a platform to new writers, and to provide opportunities for more experienced
writers to explore the limits of their craft. Through our quarterly literary journal
Lighthouse, our New Fictions series of prose pamphlets and our poetry publications,
we aim to bring new opportunities for development to writers from across the UK and
beyond. Gatehouse Press is run on a non-profit basis: all Gatehouse staff are volunteers,
and all profits go back into publishing. For more information, see our website:
http://www.gatehousepress.com

Body text set in Garamond; titles in Day Roman. Used under licence.

Special thanks to Meirion Jordan, Lee Seaman and James Higham

Cover photograph: The German Army on the Western Front, 1914-1918, © IWM
Copyright for all film stills lies with the filmmakers

Cover design by Norwich Designer
Printed and bound in the UK

Fierce Light was co-commissioned by 14-18 NOW: WW1 Centenary Art Commissions, Norfolk & Norwich Festival and Writers' Centre Norwich

Fierce Light

CONTENTS

Gatehouse Press

Foreword: On Fierce Light

Perhaps more than any other art form, the poetry of the First World War has connected succeeding generations with the horrors and complexities of that conflict, crystallising an experience unimaginable to those of us who now read these works at a century's remove. Fierce Light, a co-commission by 14-18 NOW, Norfolk & Norwich Festival and Writers' Centre Norwich, is an opportunity for artists and audiences to look afresh at the events of 100 years ago and their resonance today.

Fierce Light brings together poets and film-makers to create new works inspired by the First World War on the 100th anniversary of the Battle of the Somme, the deadliest battle in UK military history.

Each poet has responded to the commission from their own perspective of war and the history of WW1. Some have taken a personal journey into their family histories and others have looked at their own nation's engagement with the conflict. They all bring a contemporary voice to the impact of war through the ages. The pairing of a film-maker with each poet to create a filmic response adds a further artistic dimension and gives us, as audience, another way in which to experience the poems.

Fierce Light is part of 14-18 NOW, a five-year programme of arts commissions that connect us all with the First World War. We are delighted to be working in partnership with Norfolk & Norwich Festival and Writers' Centre Norwich on this collaboration, and I would particularly like to thank Chris Gribble, William Galinksy and Sam Ruddock as well as our 14-18 NOW producer Emma Dunton, for their enthusiasm and dedication. For their support, I would like to thank the Heritage Lottery Fund, Arts Council England and DCMS.

Most of all, I would like to thank the poets and film-makers for creating these powerful and moving poems and films.

— Jenny Waldman,
    Director, 14-18 NOW: WW1 Centenary Art Commissions

Introduction

The Somme – or specifically the British experience of the battle that raged in Picardy from 1st July to 18th November 1916 – has become an emblem of a war that most people now consider to have been both terrible and unnecessary. Casualty figures, numbering around 57,000 for the British on the first day alone, are apalling. The experience of the infantry, cowering in their trenches and, as summer turned to autumn, increasingly bogged down in the mud, jarred by the extraordinary noise of the artillery barrages that preceded the various assaults that made up the battle, are difficult to comprehend and convey.

Fierce Light seeks to explore the visceral, historical, personal, and communal experiences of The Battle of the Somme. How do you convey the aesthetics of the battle, and the sense of crouched horizontality that characterised trench warfare? How do you present the everyday objects that survived the war in a way that conveys a sense of the material existence of the men and women who owned and used them? How do you present the contested German, British, French and other narratives – national and imperial – side by side?

These questions and many more persist, as does the sense that humans were, and continue to be attracted to and repelled by the violence implicit in the First World War specifically, and war more generally. Yet, as historians constantly remind us, despite its horror very few people living in the majority of the combatant nations in 1916 would have argued against the notion that the First World War was anything but a patriotic war, and many would have claimed that it was also a war for ideals, fought in defence of civilisation, or culture. For most soldiers and civilians alike, the fighting on the Somme in 1916 was terrible and *necessary*, a bloody mark on the road to victory. Millions of people went to view the enduringly famous feature-length film – released in August 1916 – about the battle, and many shook their heads at what they saw, and yet the battle and the war continued around the world, and German and British soldiers returned to the Somme to fight over the very same ground in 1918.

For the British over the last century, the great and terrible Battle of the Somme has become what cultural historians define as a *lieu de mémoir* or a 'realm or site of memory'. There is no one alive with a direct memory of fighting on the Western Front in 1916: really, we have no idea what it was like to live through the battle, but somehow we think that we do, and we keep returning to it, over and over, to try to understand what happened.

Poetry and film were, and continue to be central to the development of the popular understanding of the First World War as a *lieu de mémoir*, perhaps because of their power to convey both direct and abstract experience. The poetry of, for example, Wilfred Owen, Isaac Rosenberg, Edmund Blunden and David Jones is both highly personal and, because war continues, also universal. Like the flawed but powerful *Battle the Somme* film from 1916, the poems are efforts to unpick the war, and to help others who were not there to understand it as well. Like the newly commissioned Fierce Light poetry here, and the films that have been made in response to it, these represent a creative response to the memory of a conflict that was, and remains, a personal and collective trauma.

— Dr Alisa Miller,
  Norwich University of the Arts

Fierce Light

'Hide in this battered crumbling line
Hide in these rude promiscuous graves,
Till one shall make our story shine
In the fierce Light it craves.'

'The Fierce Light'
Major John Ebenezer Stewart, M.C.

When your mother calls you, come

Yrsa Daley-Ward

There are things that you've got to do in this life.

There are things that you need to do.

If your mother was stolen
or you never had one
You go to the one who calls you
even if her voice comes through from far away
and she doesn't know your name.

Your name is
Royden. Roy for short.
Conrad, perhaps,
or Walter.
Laselle,
Lionel,
Ward,
Campbell

...where you're headed
these things hardly matter.

The morning is red
and tough as your hands.
The Sun is on your head
preparing to leave.
Everyone knows
but nobody says
Where you're headed it will hardly be.

Your uncle holds his grief in his pocket.
Keeps his thoughts buttoned up to the top
smiles so low in his throat
you wouldn't spot it.
Nods goodbye with dark eyes,
dry with hope.

Your grandma said,
"*Don't you go.*
This war that isn't ours
will take the best of us
and the worst of us
and the ones that don't deserve this
and of course
the ones who do
and the brave ones
and the foolish
what's the difference
when we lose them?

Our men too black
so they send dem away
Our men try back again
dey send dem away
Some of dem too soft
and dey run them 'way
most they a guh lose
and few they take
Why our boys a run guh foreign
to be German bait?"

But you were born
Black
and itching to see the world

Black
and cool under fire
Black
and handsome
in a suit

They wouldn't take your cousins
For reasons you don't know
Your brother stands
trembling beside you.

The motherland called from across the water.
She said *Rule Britannia*.
You heard the cry
sure as you stand here
or
sure as you don't
you paid your money
to go and to fight

and when your mother calls you
you come swiftly
come fuss-less
come full of want
and good intention
come heavy footed
come half-reciting
parables you learned
as a child
running over fields
with pans of water
quoting English
verse

but wait

one thing mother
did not say
I could be ashamed
or
I will be ashamed of you.

One thing she did not say
They wont want to fight
beside you.

One thing you were never told
Some of you wont make it all the way
you can be taken out
laying telephone poles
and there is nothing like this cold.

There will be blood on your mind,
always blood on your mind
and you are only loved back home.

and one more thing to know
one more shocker
The Somme is a bloody free-for-all,
shells love every man equally.
Shells won't point at the mud on their
faces, laugh and say
now I look like you, Sam.

Shells will catch you at mealtime
smiling in your face.
Shells will spot you through the earth

everyone burns the same.

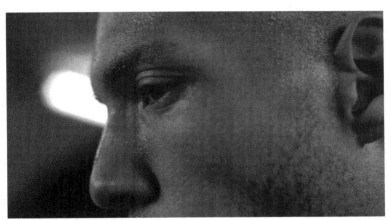

From *Paid to Fight*, a film response by Matt Kay to Yrsa Daley-Ward's 'When your mother calls you, come'

© Matt Kay

From *Paid to Fight*, a film response by Matt Kay to Yrsa Daley-Ward's 'When your mother calls you, come'

© Matt Kay

From *Paid to Fight*, a film response by Matt Kay to Yrsa Daley-Ward's 'When your mother calls you, come'

© Matt Kay

Private Joseph Kay

Jackie Kay

My grandfather — Joseph Kay, Highland Light Infantry,
After his capture on the 17th of January,

Prisoner of war, Boulon, Cambrai, and on and on
From the second battle of the Somme,

After the death of friends who did not become
Fathers, grandfathers, husbands, old sons;

Tram drivers, ship-builders, miners,
Lovers, joiner-inners– never, ever raised his voice in anger.

My father: John Kay, boy, up at dawn,
Spies his father (shy man, bit withdrawn, shrapnel in his arm)

Polishing the brass buttons of his tram driver's uniform,
Heavy, green,

In a slot-like machine,
The smell of Woodbine, shoes shined, his voice rising

Coorie Doon; if I was the man on the moon;
I'm only a rough old diamond,

Come to me Thora! And what was that Wagner aria?
Song sheets flutter. Blood, bone, air,

Ballads slide down the years, broken lines.
My father, ninety, still singing his father.

The past is lively, impossible to pin down.
There's life in the old dog yet, John pipes

Private Joseph Kay takes a long breath
Hits the sharp note, hangs on, blows out.

John Kay and Jackie Kay.

From *Private Joseph Kay*, a film response by Matt Kay to Jackie Kay's 'Private Joseph Kay'

© Matt Kay

John Kay

From *Private Joseph Kay*, a film response by Matt Kay to Jackie Kay's 'Private Joseph Kay'

© Matt Kay

Known Unto God

Bill Manhire

To you, your name also,
Did you think there was nothing but two or three
pronunciations in the sound of your name?
— Walt Whitman

Boy on horseback,
boy on a bicycle, boy all the way
from Tolaga Bay

blown to bits in a minute.

*

Once I was small bones
in my mother's body
just taking a nap.
Now my feet can't find the sap.

*

In Devil's Wood
I broke my leg and went beneath a tank.
Strange beast! Last thing I heard
was the guns all going, you know,
blankety-blankety-blank.

*

My last letter home
turned out entirely pointless.
I wrote *whizz-bang*
a dozen times

to try and say the noises.

*

Well I was here from the start, amazing...
straight off the farm at Taieri Mouth.

I lifted my head and ran like the blazes.
Went south.

*

I whistled while I could.
Then I was gone for good.

*

So strange to be underground and single
and dreaming of Dunedin.

But such a picnic!

The last thing I saw
was a tin of Ideal Milk.

*

I remember my father and my mother.
They yelled, they cursed.

My whole head hurt.

Up on the wire I couldn't hear a thing.
I who had spent my whole life listening.

*

They dug me up in Caterpillar Valley
and brought me home –
well, all of the visible bits of me.

Now people arrive at dawn and sing.
And I have a new word: *skateboarding*.

*

Not all of me is here inside.
I built Turk Lane before I died.

Kia ahatia!

*

Somewhere between Colombo and Cairo,
the ocean seemed to dip. I thought I could hear
the stamping of horses coming from it.

*

They taught me how to say *refugee*.
Then my father and mother floated away from me.

This was on the way to Lampedusa.
By now we were all at sea.

*

We were all at sea.

*

They called out while they could.
~~They called out while they could~~.

Then they were gone for good.

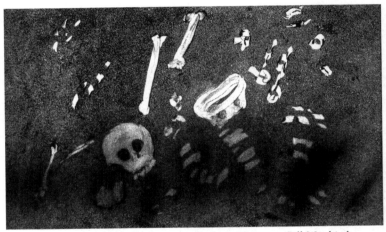

From *Known Unto God*, a film response by Suzie Hanna to Bill Manhire's 'Known Unto God'

© Suzie Hanna

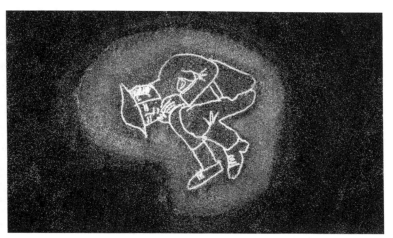

From *Known Unto God*, a film response by Suzie Hanna to Bill Manhire's
'Known Unto God'

© Suzie Hanna

July 1, 1916: With the Ulster Division

Paul Muldoon

1

You have to wonder why one old ram will step
out along a turf bank on the far side of Killeshil, his feet raw
from a bad case of rot,
while another stays hunched under his cape
of sackcloth or untreated sheepskin.
That memory's urgent as a skelf
in my big toenail, or a nick
in my own ear, drawing me back
to a bog hole where black water swirled
and our blaze-faced mare
sank to her hocks. For even as I grasped a camouflage net
hanging over the dressing station in Clairfaye Farm
I thought of the halt and lame
who, later today, must be carried along a trench

named Royal Avenue, who'll find themselves entrenched
no less physically than politically. I think now of young O'Rawe
of the Royal Irish Rifles, barely out of step
though he digs with the wrong foot. I see him on Hodge's farm
of a winter morning, the sun hinting like a tin
of bully beef from a high shelf
in the Officers' Quarters. A servant boy tugging at the hay-rick
for an armful of fodder. At least we'll be spared the back-
breaking work of late August in a flax dam, the stink unfurled
like a banner across the moor
where great-coated bodies ret.
I think of Giselle, her flaxen hair in a net,
who served me last week in a village café, teaching me the Game
of the Goose even as she plucked a gander's cape.

2

At a table in Giselle's café one orderly was painting a landscape
in yellow ochre, raw sienna and raw
umber, pausing once in a while to gnaw at a tranche
of thick-skinned Camembert. Something about that estaminet
where I had tried a soupcon of gin
from an eggcup made of delf
made me intolerably homesick.
The music the orderly played on the Victrola was Offenbach's
Overture from *Orpheus In the Underworld*.
It was as if a servant girl from Vermeer
was pouring milk to steep
the bread for panady, Giselle lighting my cigarette
as Hodge himself once set a flame
to a paraffin lamp in the cowshed on that valuable farm

of land in Kileeshil. Later this morning I'll shoulder my firearm
and fall in as a raw
recruit with the veterans who followed the Boers from the Cape
of Good Hope to the Orange Free State like rats
following the Pied Piper of Hamelin
in search of gold and pelf.
That officer from the Rifles carried a blackthorn stick.
The wound in his back
brought to mind a poppy, of all things. Something has curled
up and died in the quagmire
of the trench
named Sandy Row down which the boys will surely step
on the Twelfth of July. It's a shame
it was only last week I met Giselle and fell into her amorous net.

3

You have to wonder at the zeal with which some drive a bayonet
through a straw-
stuffed effigy of Lundy. It'll be no distance to Clairfaye Farm
from Thiepval Wood. It'll be one step
forward into No-Man's-Land between the Ghibbelines
and Guelphs
with their little bags of tricks, *ich, ich* –
one step forward, two steps back
towards the Schwaben Redoubt. I noticed how O'Rawe twirled
his mustache as he sang Tom Moore's
'Let Erin Remember.' Commanding officers in sheepskin capes
are under orders not to leave the trench
and go over the top. It's the duty of the rest of us to seek fame
and fortune. The needle had stuck in a rut

on the Victrola halfway through a foxtrot.
The blaze-faced mare Hodge bought from a farmer in Ardstraw,
the ram from a farmer in Tydavnet.
It seems now everywhere I go there's a trench
that's precisely as tall and thin
as my own good self
and through which, if I march double quick,
I may yet find my way back
to bounteous Killeeshil, the bog from which I was hurled
into this bog. There's a strong chance that Giselle, mon amour,
will hold me hostage in my bed at Clairfaye Farm
and simply not allow me to escape.
For the moment I must concentrate on taking aim
as I adjust my helmet and haversack and mount the firing step.

From *July 1, 1916: With the Ulster Division*, a film response by George Belfield to Paul Muldoon's 'July 1, 1916: With the Ulster Division'

© George Belfield

From *July 1, 1916: With the Ulster Division*, a film response by George Belfield to Paul Muldoon's 'July 1, 1916: With the Ulster Division'

© George Belfield

On your 'A 1940 Memory'

Daljit Nagra

Not one of your Somme poems,
yet Sassoon, you'll end up there.
From a 1940 afternoon of war's
worst troubles, you're caught
by a clouded yellow butterfly.
You claim you're marked by it;
that its loveliness is a scorch
when suffering is everywhere.

The poem written years' after
your day like a dream-hunter
who stalks a loitering butterfly.
The freighted gain of each step
in a sunless mid-September
invokes in me your youthful ire
for the Somme's sunlit picture
of hell. No wonder you state
how Time will blur the pain.

Dear Jack, what blurs you most
so great words forever moral
your mind to war recall?
Is it the soldier smithereens
at your arm, the Hun dispersed
by your pluck that day you lay
in their bunker to read sonnets?
Or how you just couldn't die?

Look at you now, our haunted
hero. Perhaps an image of Britain,
whose kin made a killing in India,
who chases from his country
home a clouded yellow butterfly
that's gone off course to recover
a sunny afternoon of Empire.

From *Across Fields*, a film response by Tim Davies to Daljit Nagra's 'On Your 'A 1940 Memory"

© Tim Davies

Afterword: On Film Poems

Poetry films have become increasingly popular in the 21st century, from web viewing to vast architectural projections, curated gallery exhibitions, conferences and festival screenings. Lucy English, poet, and creator of the Liberated Words film festival, recognises that 'as a poet it can be challenge to "let go" of control of the final outcome.' But that 'a good poetry film is not just an "illustration" of a poem, it is the melding of word and image which creates a separate experience.'

We are multi-sensory people. When text meets visual art, conditions are created for comprehensive immersion in the subject, and powerful engagements between past and present. New York artist Jenny Holzer's permanent installation of towering animated lights in the lobby of the new 7 World Trade Centre building at Ground Zero is comprised of historical scrolling texts about New York by over a dozen poets and writers. In this busy public space, metres from where the Twin Towers once stood, the urban crowd can read and reflect on the literary history of the city as they pause for thought, remembrance, or walk on. Her collaborations with poet Henri Cole include Blur, a love sonnet sequence simultaneously projected onto the Guggenheim Museum in Venice and the police station opposite, the latter building a reminder to Venetians of Mussolini's secret police operations. The projections spilled across the canal, animated by the water's surface, the viewer placed inside the poem as enveloping landscape.

Animator Ruth Lingford collaborated with the writer Sara Maitland to create Pleasures of War (1998), a film which references the Biblical story of Judith and Holofernes to graphically portray links between war and sexual desire. A violent history of war is represented in Lingford's bold morphing style, collaging archive film footage of WW1 armies with stark illustrations redolent of Kathe Kollwitz's woodcuts. The animator, like a poet, uses dynamic composition, varied scale and clear ideograms in the creation of powerful metaphors.

Bill Manhire's poem 'Known Unto God' sparks a massive emotional charge for me. The voices of the Dead are young, innocent, arriving at or fleeing war in good faith. The poem seems to be located in the grim archaeology of the mud of the Somme, moving out to sea with the 21st century's migrant drownings. Stella Duffy's vocal interpretation of those voices in the film conveys the arbitrary sudden nature of brutal death, 'kia ahatia' translating as 'so what?' Close reading brings terminal colloquial phrases into sharp relief, 'gone for good', these are those Glorious Dead, dying for ideals.

My decision to animate mud and raw pigments in response to the poem comes from knowledge of my own grandfather's experiences at the Somme, and from images of the blasted terrain, including locations mentioned in the poem such as 'Devil's Wood'. The naive drawing style is in sympathy with the youth of the victims, literally scratching out glimpses from the text, but leaving space for the viewer to hear and consider the poem. Creating a visual shape to reflect, frame and communicate the spirit of the text whilst avoiding literal illustration, as Lucy English warns, is the challenge for the poetry filmmaker.

— Prof Suzie Hanna,
  Norwich University of the Arts

Biographical Notes

Yrsa Daley-Ward is a writer and poet of mixed West Indian and West African heritage. Born to a Jamaican mother and a Nigerian father, Yrsa was raised by her devout Seventh Day Adventist grandparents in the small town of Chorley in the North of England. Her first collection of stories *On Snakes and Other Stories* was published by 3:AM Press.

Jackie Kay was born and brought up in Scotland. She has published five collections of poetry for adults (*The Adoption Papers* won the Forward Prize, a Saltire Award and a Scottish Arts Council Book Award) and several for children. She was awarded an MBE in 2006.

Bill Manhire (b. 1946) grew up in small country pubs at the bottom of New Zealand's South Island. He was educated at the University of Otago and at University College London, where he almost became an Old Norse scholar. For many years he taught at Victoria University, where he founded the International Institute of Modern Letters, home to New Zealand's leading creative writing program. Bill was New Zealand's inaugural Poet Laureate. His most recent collections are the prize-winning *Lifted*, *The Victims of Lightning*, and a *Selected Poems*. He has also published short fiction, most of which was recently collected in *The Stories of Bill Manhire* (VUP, 2015).

Biographical Notes

Paul Muldoon is one of Ireland's leading contemporary poets, along with being a professor of poetry, an editor, critic and translator. The author of twelve major collections of poetry, he has also published innumerable smaller collections, works of criticism, opera libretti, books for children, song lyrics and radio and television drama. His poetry has been translated into twenty languages and has won numerous awards. Muldoon served as Professor of Poetry at Oxford University from 1999 to 2004. He has taught at Princeton University since 1987 and currently occupies the Howard G.B. Clark '21 chair in the Humanities. He has been poetry editor of *The New Yorker* since 2007.

Daljit Nagra was born and raised in West London, then Sheffield. He currently lives in Harrow with his wife and daughters and works in a secondary school. His first collection, *Look We Have Coming to Dover!*, won the 2007 Forward Prize for Best First Collection and was shortlisted for the Costa Poetry Award. In 2008 he won the South Bank Show/Arts Council Decibel Award. *Tippoo Sultan's Incredible White-Man-Eating Tiger Toy-Machine!!!* was shortlisted for the T. S. Eliot Prize 2011.

Note of Thanks

In preparing Fierce Light for publication, Gatehouse Press would like to acknowledge the support and encouragement of the poets Yrsa Daley-Ward, Jackie Kay, Bill Manhire, Paul Muldoon, and Daljit Nagra; the filmmakers George Belfield, Tim Davies, Suzie Hanna, and Matthew Kay; 14-18 NOW (Emma Dunton, Pak Ling Wan and Jenny Waldman); the Imperial War Museums (Charlotte Czyzyk, Madeleine James, Sophy Moynagh, Nigel Steel and Alan Wakefield); Norfolk & Norwich Festival (William Galinsky, Mark Denbigh, Lis Jennings and their teams); Writers' Centre Norwich (Chris Gribble, Alice Kent, Jonathan Morley, Sam Ruddock and their teams); and The Cogency (Selina Ocean and Janice White).

At Gatehouse, particular thanks are due to Dr Meirion Jordan, Andrew McDonnell and Sam Ruddock in editing and producing this publication.

Acknowledgements

Fierce Light was commissioned by 14-18 NOW: WW1 Centenary Art Commissions, Norfolk & Norwich Festival and Writers' Centre Norwich

Fierce Light was first exhibited at East Gallery[NUA], Norwich, in May 2016, as part of Norfolk & Norwich Festival.

14-18 NOW: WW1 Centenary Art Commissions is supported by the National Lottery through the Arts Council England and the Heritage Lottery Fund and by the Department for Culture, Media and Sport.

This publication and exhibition are part of the Norwich University of the Arts' 'Created and Contested Territories' research programme.